ON THE WAY
TO BETHLEHEM:
LEADER GUIDE

On the Way to Bethlehem
An Advent Study

On the Way to Bethlehem

978-1-7910-3328-6

978-1-7910-3330-9 *eBook*

On the Way to Bethlehem DVD

978-1-7910-3332-3

On the Way to Bethlehem Leader Guide

978-1-7910-3329-3

978-1-7910-3331-6 *eBook*

ON THE WAY TO

BETHLEHEM

AN ADVENT STUDY

ROB FUQUAY

Abingdon Press | Nashville

On the Way to Bethlehem
An Advent Study
Leader Guide

Copyright © 2024 Abingdon Press
All rights reserved.

978-1-7910-3329-3

MANUFACTURED IN THE UNITED STATES OF AMERICA

CONTENTS

INTRODUCTION

In *On the Way to Bethlehem*, Rev. Rob Fuquay, senior pastor of St. Luke's United Methodist Church (Indianapolis) plans a four-stop spiritual itinerary for readers to enrich their observation and celebration of the Advent season.

The journey toward Christmas on which Rob leads readers begins in Rome, the seat of supreme political power in the first century; continues to Jerusalem, Israel's holiest city; goes through Nazareth, a village so seemingly inconsequential it is unknown in first-century literature outside of the New Testament; and ends in Bethlehem, where Christians believe the Sovereign God became flesh in a baby cradled in a manger among those the world deems little and least.

As leader of a small group in your congregation or other community studying Rob's book, you are an important part of this Advent journey. You will use the session plans in this Leader Guide to prepare four sessions (with an optional fifth session) for adult learners:

- Session 1: Rome: A Place of Longing
  Our journey begins in Rome, where human political and economic power was most concentrated in the first century—yet where those same human forces evoked divine longings that God would meet in the birth of Jesus. What do we long for? How does Jesus meet those longings? How do we discern ways in which God is meeting our longings now?

- Session 2: Jerusalem: A Place of Waiting
  In Jerusalem, devout worshippers waited for Zechariah the
  priest to bless them at the Temple. Zechariah and his wife,
  Elizabeth, had just received an unexpected promise after
  years of their own waiting. For what do we wait today?
  How and why do we feel "barren" in our lives? How
  can seasons of waiting deepen our faith in God and our
  faithful response?

- Session 3: Nazareth: A Place of Simplicity
  The small village of Nazareth was a place where life was
  likely much slower and simpler than in more worldly
  places like neighboring Sepphoris. Into just such
  simplicity, however, an angel brought a young woman
  news of God's world-changing action. How can we
  simplify our lives? How can we "carry Jesus within"
  ourselves, nurturing the Word becoming flesh in everyday
  ways?

- Session 4: Bethlehem: A Place of Humility
  The "little town of Bethlehem" was indeed a small and
  humble place. But as God so often chooses the small and
  humble, God chose Bethlehem to be the birthplace of
  God's Son. How do lessons from Bethlehem's history in
  God's story with Israel help us become people who both
  receive and give blessings in our world today?

- Session 5 (Optional): Persia: A Place of Return
  Anyone can come back home after a journey. But coming
  back "a different way" is something we must be intentional
  about, and "re-turning" to a new and different life that
  God has opened for us can only be done in dependence on
  God's power. How is God calling us to "re-turn," repent,
  and offer gifts of value to others?

Most groups will use this resource to study *On the Way to Bethlehem* as a part of their Advent observations, but nothing prevents you from using it at other times.

This leader's guide contains scriptures and quotations from Rob's book, allowing you to use it on its own. However, you and your learners will benefit from it most if you use it while reading *On the Way to Bethlehem*.

Each session contains the following elements to draw from:

- Session Goals
- Biblical Foundations—Scripture texts for the session, in the New Revised Standard Version Updated Edition.
- Before Your Session—Practical suggestions for preparing a productive session.
- Starting Your Session—Discussion questions intended to "warm up" your group for fruitful discussion.
- Watch Session Video—You may choose to use the accompanying DVD or streaming video (available through Amplify Media) to enhance your sessions.
- Book Discussion Questions—You likely will not be able or want to use all the questions in every session, so feel free to pick and choose based on your group's interests and the Spirit's leading.
- Closing Your Session—A focused discussion or reflection, often suggesting action to take beyond the session.
- Opening and Closing Prayers—Use these prayers as printed, or allow them to inspire your own prepared or extemporaneous prayers.
- Optional Extensions—One or more ways to continue discussion about or engage in action related to the session's topics and themes.

Although this leader guide largely assumes groups will be meeting in-person, it does provide some tips for groups meeting in virtual or in hybrid settings. With some creative thought, you can adapt your sessions as needed.

Thank you for your willingness to lead adult learners in studying *On the Way to Bethlehem*. May you and your group experience a meaningful and joyful journey toward a richer and fuller celebration of Jesus's birth.

SESSION 1
ROME
A Place of Longing

Session Goals

This session's readings, reflection, discussion, and prayer will help participants:

- Reflect on their experiences of and insights gained from journeys they have taken.
- Review characteristics of the Roman Empire that shaped Jewish people's experience in the first century.
- Understand how Roman rule shaped Jewish longings in Jesus's day, and how the authority and impact of modern "Romes" can shape deep longings now.
- Identify possible indications of God's activity in the world and in their lives.
- Appreciate the metaphors Paul uses to discuss present suffering, future hope, and present waiting in Romans 8:18-25.
- Identify practical actions they can take about social issues that concern them as willing participants in God's activity in the world.

Biblical Foundations

In those days a decree went out from Caesar Augustus that all the world should be registered. This was the first registration and was taken while Quirinius was governor of Syria. All went to their own towns to be registered.

Luke 2:1-3

I consider that the sufferings of this present time are not worth comparing with the glory about to be revealed to us. For the creation waits with eager longing for the revealing of the children of God, for the creation was subjected to futility, not of its own will, but by the will of the one who subjected it, in hope that the creation itself will be set free from its enslavement to decay and will obtain the freedom of the glory of the children of God. We know that the whole creation has been groaning together as it suffers together the pains of labor, and not only the creation, but we ourselves, who have the first fruits of the Spirit, groan inwardly while we wait for adoption, the redemption of our bodies. For in hope we were saved. Now hope that is seen is not hope, for who hopes for what one already sees? But if we hope for what we do not see, we wait for it with patience.

Romans 8:18-25

Before Your Session

- Carefully and prayerfully read this session's Biblical Foundations, more than once. Note words and phrases that attract your attention and meditate on them. Write down questions you have, and try to answer them, consulting trusted Bible commentaries. Become as familiar with these scriptures as possible.

- Carefully read the introduction and chapter 1 of *On the Way to Bethlehem*, more than once so you are familiar with the content.

- You will need: Bibles for in-person participants and/or screen slides prepared with Scripture texts for sharing (identify the translation used); newsprint or a markerboard and markers (for in-person sessions).

- If using the DVD or streaming video, preview the session 1 video segment. Choose the best time in your session plan for viewing it.

- Secure and prepare a comfortable meeting space for your group, easily accessible to all participants regardless of physical ability. If meeting virtually or using a hybrid format, be sure to test your teleconferencing platform and other audiovisual technology before every session.

- *Optional*: Place an Advent wreath with four candles in your meeting space where all may see it (whether they are in person or online).

- *Optional*: Obtain or prepare a map of the first-century Roman Empire and mark these places: Rome, Jerusalem, Nazareth, and Bethlehem. (If you will be using the optional fifth session, you may also want to make sure your map shows these locations in relation to Persia [modern Iran].) Display this map in your meeting space where all participants (in person or online) may see it, and/or prepare to distribute the map on paper copies or electronically.

Starting Your Session

Welcome participants. Express your excitement for your group's shared study of *On the Way to Bethlehem* by Rob Fuquay this Advent season. Talk briefly about your interest in the book and this study and invite volunteers to do the same.

Invite volunteers to discuss briefly the "biggest" trip they've ever taken—however they'd like to define "biggest." As needed, encourage discussion with such questions as:

- Where did you go and why?
- What advance preparations did you make—and were they enough?
- What was the most surprising, memorable, or challenging thing about your journey?
- What things(s), tangible or intangible, did you bring back from your journey?
- How, if at all, are you different because of your journey?

Ask:

- Why, as Rob writes, do people frequently speak of the spiritual life as a journey? Does this image resonate with your spirituality or faith? Why or why not?

Tell participants this study is a scriptural and spiritual "journey" to four destinations associated with the Christmas story: Rome, Jerusalem, Nazareth, and Bethlehem. (If you are displaying a map of the first-century Roman Empire, point out these places now.) Invite participants to talk briefly about any associations they already have with any or all of these places. You may wish to write responses on newsprint or markerboard for future reference.

Read aloud from Rob's book: "What we gain from all these places will be different for each person, and different even for ourselves over time. If we took this same journey every year, what we take from it would not be the same, because we change. God speaks to us where we are, and where we are this Advent is different from any Advent in our lives."

Opening Prayer

Optional: Light the first candle (wax or electric) in your group's Advent wreath.

Lead this prayer or one in your own words:

O God, from the beginning you have called your people to undertake a journey in faith. As we begin our study this Advent, guide us to you—through our reading of and reflection on Scripture, through our speaking and listening, through our fellowship, and through the presence of your Holy Spirit. May our time together be a journey that brings us closer to Jesus Christ, whose first coming we celebrate, whose future coming we await, and who promises to take us on a journey that will not end even in death. Amen.

Watch Session Video

Watch the session 1 video segment together. Discuss:

- Which of Rob's statements most interested, intrigued, surprised, or confused you? Why?
- What questions does this video segment raise for you?

Book Discussion Questions

Rome, Then and Now

Invite volunteers to talk briefly about what they know about the Roman Empire—from their time in school, from their reading, from media and popular culture.

Recruit a volunteer to read aloud Luke 2:1-3. Discuss:

- How does the emperor's decree affect the lives of his subjects?

- What practical purposes does the decree serve?
- How does the decree serve to assert Roman power and authority?

Summarize these points from this section of chapter 1:

- In Jesus's day, "Rome was the center of the major Empire that wrapped around the Mediterranean Sea."
- The Empire was governed by the emperor and the Roman Senate.
- The Empire spread advancements in construction, engineering, and social services through Europe, North Africa, and Asia Minor (the peninsula that is today Turkey).
- "The *Pax Romana* started under Augustus brought unprecedented peace and prosperity to Roman citizens, but for occupied lands like Israel the experience was different."
- Rome started ruling Israel (Judea) in 63BC, maintaining a strong military occupation presence and enforcing its rule through local "client-kings" obedient to the Empire.
- The Empire showed little sensitivity to Jewish religious convictions.
- Herod the Great was Rome's client-king when Jesus was born. Herod was Jewish by birth, but associated with the non-Jewish Roman elite and was notorious for abusing his power and eliminating threats to his position—even family members.

Discuss:

- Rob points out the Roman Empire had "power to do good things," but "not everything about Roman occupation was good." What would you list as positives and negatives about Roman rule? Do you think one outweighs the other? Why or why not?

- As those living in a conquered and occupied land, Jewish people in Jesus's day were "second-class citizens," writes Rob, or "noncitizens," without voice or vote. Review the examples Rob relates of how Rome treated its Jewish subjects. Which do you think were especially offensive or oppressive, and why?
- Have you ever been or felt like a second-class citizen? What happened (or is happening)? What groups of people are treated as second-class citizens or noncitizens in the country where you live, and why?
- "Rome is that place where decisions impact your life beyond your control." As Rob asks, "When is the last time you were affected by some decree in Rome?" What about your family? Your local community? Your congregation?
- Even as various "Romes" affect us all, as Rob explains, "Some of us live in Rome." Where and how, if at all, are you in a position to make decisions that affect the lives of other people, especially those far away?
- Under Roman rule, writes Rob, all the Jewish people could do "was long for something better." In which aspects of your life are you longing for "something better?" What longings do your family, community, and congregation feel most keenly?
- Rob asks readers to consider "the longings of God." For what do you believe God longs? Why? How do we discern when and whether our longings are in alignment with God's?
- Human longings sometimes go unfulfilled. Can or do God's longings? Why?

God Is Always Directing

Discuss:

- Rob compares God's activity to water evaporating from the earth's surface to form rain clouds: "By the time we see convincing evidence of God's activity, the heavy lifting by God has been done." When, if ever, was a time you saw what you consider "convincing evidence" of God at work in the world? In your life? What "heavy lifting" had to have taken place in order to bring about that visible sign of God's action?

- Do you agree visible signs can confirm but not create faith? Why or why not?

- When, if ever, has seeing signs of God's hand at work challenged your faith, as Rob says seeing such signs can? How did or how could you handle that challenge?

- Rob quotes Dr. Fred Craddock as saying faith is more about past realities than future hope. What do you understand these words to mean? Do you agree with them? Why or why not?

Groanings and Birth Pains

Recruit a volunteer to read aloud Romans 8:18-25. Discuss:

- What do you identify as "the sufferings of this present time" (verse 18)? How do you describe Paul's attitude toward them?

- For what does Paul say the whole creation is waiting (verse 19)? How does (or how could) considering evidence of "futility" and "decay" as signs of creation's waiting affect your relationship to the natural world?

- How does Paul's "sudden shift" of metaphors in verse 22 put our and creation's suffering into a new context? What do you think about describing these sufferings as the pains of labor and childbirth?

- In verse 23, Paul shifts metaphors again, to speak of "adoption." What does this image suggest about the future for which we and creation are waiting?

- What are "the first fruits of the Spirit" Paul says we have even now? Why don't these fruits keep us from groaning inwardly (see also 8:26-27)?

- Paul says we await "the redemption of our bodies." How does or should this conviction shape Christians' attitudes toward their bodies?

- Rob quotes David Williamson: "[H]eaven does not decree... God births." What distinction is Williamson drawing? What does it tell us about who God is and how God works in the world? What implications does it have for those who operate (or who would rather operate) by decree?

- What does Paul mean by "hope" (verses 24-25)? What is the relationship of patience to hope?

- Rob suggests that starting the Christmas story in Rome keeps us from treating it as a "tonic" or a "warm fuzzy." How so? Do you agree? Why or why not?

- "Any of us who care at all about the affairs of this world and the people who lead countries, counties, and communities are routinely challenged to consider whether we are putting our faith in Rome or God." How do you honestly discern the answer to this challenge?

Closing Your Session

Read aloud from Rob's book: "[W]hen our hearts break over the things that break God's heart, God may call us to be solutions to the problems.... God doesn't reveal God's will to people without making a way."

Ask volunteers to identify social issues that trouble them. In his book, Rob mentions the issues of gun violence; mental health; inequities in health care; housing; education; and climate change as possibilities. Your group's members may express concern about any of these or other issues. List responses on newsprint or markerboard.

Invite participants to form small groups of two to three people each. Direct each group to help each member identify at least one practical action they have not already taken that they could take to involve themselves in God's activity in the world. Encourage the small groups to decide on how their members will hold each other accountable for following through on one or more of the identified actions.

Note: If you are leading an especially small group, you can lead such a discussion with all participants.

Close by reading aloud from Rob's book: "Most of the radical revolutions in history have started with the troubled spirits of individuals who long for a better world, individuals who usually feel inadequate to be change agents but who act upon their troubling."

Thank participants for their engagement in this session. Encourage them to read chapter 2 of *On the Way to Bethlehem* before your next session.

Closing Prayer

Sovereign God, empires rise and fall, but your good purposes remain. As you called your saints in the past to challenge the powers of this world with the power of your justice and love, so you call us. We know we cannot change this world on our own. We also know we cannot change it without you. In Jesus Christ, you reveal your will and join us to him so we may participate in bringing it about. This Advent season, grant us courage and trust to do so, in his name. Amen.

Optional Extensions

- Rob discusses how he spent his first Christmas away from home in Bethlehem. When and where did you spend your first Christmas away from home? What was the experience like? Has it affected your observation of Christmas in any lasting ways?

- Recruit interested volunteers to research what historians know about Herod the Great from sources outside the Bible, and invite them to report back to the full group at the start of your next session. What connections can your group make between Herod as known to academic history and as he is presented in Matthew 2?

- One privilege and responsibility Christians living in America have that Jewish people living in first-century occupied Judea did not have is the privilege and responsibility of participating in a representative democracy. How seriously do you and your congregation take opportunities for civic engagement? How do these opportunities express your faith? As a group, write postcards or letters to your elected officials to make your voice as people of faith heard about issues you think are important.

SESSION 2
JERUSALEM
A Place of Waiting

Session Goals

This session's readings, reflection, discussion, and prayer will help participants:

- Identify their special, "once-in-a-lifetime" experiences and connect them to Zechariah's once-in-a-lifetime encounter with the angel Gabriel.
- Understand basics about the history of the Temple Mount and Temple in Jerusalem so they can more deeply appreciate the setting of the announcement of John the Baptist's birth.
- Reflect on their experiences of feeling barren and of waiting on God, and how these experiences might deepen faith and serve God's larger purposes.
- Practice keeping silence as an Advent discipline.

Biblical Foundation

In the days of King Herod of Judea, there was a priest named Zechariah, who belonged to the priestly order of Abijah. His wife was descended from the daughters of Aaron, and her name was Elizabeth. Both of them were righteous before God, living blamelessly according to all the commandments and regulations of the Lord. But they had no children because Elizabeth was barren, and both were getting on in years.

Once when he was serving as priest before God during his section's turn of duty, he was chosen by lot, according to the custom of the priesthood, to enter the sanctuary of the Lord to offer incense. Now at the time of the incense offering, the whole assembly of the people was praying outside. Then there appeared to him an angel of the Lord, standing at the right side of the altar of incense. When Zechariah saw him, he was terrified, and fear overwhelmed him. But the angel said to him, "Do not be afraid, Zechariah, for your prayer has been heard. Your wife Elizabeth will bear you a son, and you will name him John. You will have joy and gladness, and many will rejoice at his birth, for he will be great in the sight of the Lord. He must never drink wine or strong drink; even before his birth he will be filled with the Holy Spirit. He will turn many of the people of Israel to the Lord their God. With the spirit and power of Elijah he will go before him, to turn the hearts of parents to their children and the disobedient to the wisdom of the righteous, to make ready a people prepared for the Lord." Zechariah said to the angel, "How can I know that this will happen? For I am an old man, and my wife is getting on in years." The angel replied, "I am Gabriel. I stand in the presence of God, and I have been sent to speak to you and to bring you this good news. But now, because you did not believe my words, which will be fulfilled in their time, you will become mute, unable to speak, until the day these things occur."

Meanwhile the people were waiting for Zechariah and wondering at his delay in the sanctuary. When he did come out, he was unable to speak to them, and they realized that he had seen a vision in the sanctuary. He kept motioning to them and remained unable to speak.

Luke 1:5-22

Before Your Session

- Carefully and prayerfully read this session's Biblical Foundations, more than once. Note words and phrases that attract your attention and meditate on them. Write down questions you have, and try to answer them, consulting trusted Bible commentaries. Become as familiar with these scriptures as possible.

- Carefully read chapter 2 of *On the Way to Bethlehem*, more than once so you are familiar with the content.

- You will need: Bibles for in-person participants and/ or screen slides prepared with Scripture texts for sharing (identify the translation used); newsprint or a markerboard and markers (for in-person sessions).

- If using the DVD or streaming video, preview the session 2 video segment. Choose the best time in your session plan for viewing it.

- If meeting virtually or using a hybrid format, be sure to test your teleconferencing platform and other audiovisual technology before the session.

Starting Your Session

Welcome participants. Ask volunteers to talk about the biggest "once-in-a-lifetime" event they've ever experienced, and/or to name an item from their "bucket lists" (things they would like to do or experience before they die). You may wish to write responses on the newsprint or markerboard.

Tell participants that Rob begins chapter 2 of his book by describing an especially memorable and dramatic "once-in-a-lifetime kind of day" he once had in Jerusalem and that the scripture your group will read and study today is about an even more memorable and dramatic "once-in-a-lifetime kind of day" in Jerusalem.

Opening Prayer

Optional: Light the first and second candles (wax or electric) in your group's Advent wreath.

Lead this prayer or one in your own words:

We cannot demand once-in-a-lifetime experiences from you, O God. But we ask that in this time of study, your Spirit would make us so aware of your wisdom, your will, and your love that we would know we have been in your presence—and, so knowing, live more moments in our lives as moments in which we expect memorable encounters with you. We make our bold prayer in the name of Jesus Christ. Amen.

Watch Session Video

Watch the session 2 video segment together. Discuss:

- Which of Rob's statements most interested, intrigued, surprised, or confused you? Why?
- What questions does this video segment raise for you?

Book Discussion Questions

Jerusalem and Its Temple

Summarize Rob's history of the site of the Temple in Jerusalem, making these points:

- King Solomon built the Temple on Mount Moriah, where there was a stone threshing floor his father, King David, had purchased to build an altar to God (2 Samuel 24:18-25; 2 Chronicles 3:1). Mount Moriah thus became the Temple Mount.

- Abraham had almost sacrificed his son on a mountain in "the land of Moriah" (Genesis 22:2).
- The Temple's Most Holy Place (Holy of Holies), which housed the Ark of the Covenant (the box containing the Ten Commandments), may have been built on the "Foundation Stone," the site of Abraham's near-sacrifice and of the threshing floor.
- Babylonian forces destroyed the Temple in 586 BC. Those who returned after the Babylonian Exile finished rebuilding the Temple in 515 BC.
- King Herod the Great rebuilt and expanded the Temple during his rule to win approval from his subjects and praise from Rome.
- Rome destroyed the Second Temple in AD 70. The Western Wall is all that remains, and it is Judaism's holiest site.
- Today, the Al-Aqsa Mosque and Dome of the Rock stand on the Temple Mount. Islam teaches that the prophet Muhammad ascended into heaven from the Foundation Stone during his visionary "Night Journey."[1]

Discuss:

- "To understand the importance of the Temple," writes Rob, "is to tell the story of Jerusalem." How so?
- Why is the Temple Mount so significant to Judaism, Christianity, and Islam?
- What places, if any, do you regard as especially meaningful, even holy? Why?

---

1   "Dome of the Rock," https://www.britannica.com/topic/Dome-of-the-Rock.

- How does Luke starting his Gospel with the story of a priest serving at the Temple in Jerusalem show Jesus's continuity with Judaism?

Recruit volunteers to read aloud Luke 1:5-22, taking the roles of the narrator, Zechariah, and Gabriel. Discuss:

- What does Luke tell us about Elizabeth and Zechariah (verses 5-7)? Why does he want us to know these things about them from the start of his story?
- Rob describes the approach to the Temple in Jerusalem and its Court of the Gentiles, of Women, of the Israelites, and of the Priests. (You might want to look at artists' reconstructions in trusted study Bibles or other Bible study resources.) What messages might the Temple's architecture and design have communicated about Israel's God and this God's people? What messages do you think the architecture and design of your congregation's building communicate—consciously or unconsciously—about God and about your congregation?
- Why and how do the long-shot odds of Zechariah's chance to enter the Holy Place matter to our understanding of what he experiences?
- Rob identifies "three important items" that would have been in the Holy Place Zechariah entered: the Bread of the Presence (see Exodus 25:30; Leviticus 24:5-9), the Lampstand (a golden menorah; see Exodus 25:31-40; Leviticus 24:1-4), and the Altar of Incense (see Exodus 30:1-10). What can you tell about the significance of these items, from the scriptures cited and from Rob's explanations? What items in your congregation's worship space would you identify as most important, and why?

- Do you find Zechariah's terrified reaction to the angel's appearance (verses 11-12) "mildly humorous," as Rob does? Why or why not?
- Rob asks, "Is it possible to carry out religious rituals and lose any expectation of experiencing God?" How do you answer, and why?

Feeling Barren and Delayed

Discuss:

- Why was childlessness often a cause for concern and sorrow in ancient Israel? In your experience, how much stigma does childlessness carry for couples, and especially women, in society today? Why?
- Rob suggests "barren" (verse 7) is "more than a physical description" of Zechariah and Elizabeth, but also "an emotional and even spiritual one." Do you agree? Why or why not?
- How does the angel's message to Zechariah (verses 13-17) address the barren waiting Elizabeth and Zechariah have been feeling?
- How is the promise to Elizabeth and Zechariah like and unlike the promises given to Abraham and Sarah (see Genesis 17:15-21; 18:9-15), Jacob and Rachel (Genesis 30:1-24), and Hannah and Elkanah (1 Samuel 1:1-20)?
- What is the significance of the angel identifying himself to Zechariah as Gabriel (verse 19; compare Daniel 8:15-17; 9:20-23)?
- "Have you ever felt barren?" asks Rob. How do you respond? If you have, how did you handle (or how are you handling) your feelings of barrenness?

- Read Rob's summary of the Hasidic parable of the Sorrow Tree. What do you think about this parable? Would you trade your sorrows for someone else's? Why or why not?
- "In the end our sorrows, like blessings, are part of who we are." How have your sorrows shaped you?
- Why does Rob call Jerusalem a place of waiting—"a stop [on the journey to Christmas] of indefinite length?" When was a time you have been waiting for something or someone longer than you would like? How do you deal with such waiting?

A Muted Blessing?

Discuss:

- Rob says for a long time he considered Zechariah's muteness (verse 20) "an unfair part of the story." Do you think it unfair? Why or why not? What, if anything, does Zechariah's reaction tell us about him? What, if anything, does it tell us about God?
- Rob says he knows "what it's like to lose hope," but "not lose faith." What would you say is the distinction between the two?
- When, if ever, has faith "become a matter of going through the motions" for you? How did you handle that time? Can "going through the motions" of faithful living ever be a positive, or is it always a negative, and why?
- Read the story Rob tells about the woman in the congregation he serves who served as a hospitality volunteer after her husband's death. Why does Rob say, of her experience, "Sometimes just showing up is a courageous act of faith?" Have you ever "just shown up" in courageous faith? What happened?

- Rob suggests, "The key to finding meaning in our waiting is to ask how our longing fits into God's bigger purpose." When, if ever, have you looked back on a time of lost hope or waiting on God to discover how it has served some larger purpose?

Closing Your Session

Rob wonders if, when Zechariah returned to priestly duties after John's birth, he did so with "deeper conviction" because of his enforced silence: "Spending a season listening to the voice of God will do that." Discuss:

- When, if ever, have you reengaged your faith with deeper conviction after a season of listening for God?
- What form(s) did your listening for God take? What did you hear? How did it change you?
- How, if at all, is your season of listening still having an effect on you?

Rob suggests Advent is "a good season to practice silence." Invite participants to sit in reflective and prayerful silence for a length of time you choose. Some groups may find a full minute of silence challenging, while others will be able to keep silence longer. Reassure participants you will keep an eye on the clock! Suggest some ways of listening for God in this silence, such as:

- Silent repetition of a word or phrase from this session's Bible story.
- Reviewing the events of their day for signs of God's presence and activity.
- Visualizing people for whom and concerns about which they are praying.

- Listening deeply to the sounds in the space around them.

After the silence, invite volunteers to talk briefly about their experience of it.

Thank participants for their engagement in this session. Encourage them to read chapter 3 of *On the Way to Bethlehem* before your next session.

Closing Prayer

Holy God, your loving faithfulness can catch us by surprise. Sometimes, we forget or take for granted your graciousness. Sometimes, we fail to expect you to take action. Sometimes, you act in ways we would never have imagined or dreamed. May your Spirit help us always to meet the surprises you have for us in faith and hope, trusting you will use them to draw us closer to yourself, through your Son, Jesus Christ. Amen.

Optional Extensions

- Continue reading the story of John the Baptist's birth in Luke 1:23-25, 57-66. How do both Elizabeth and Zechariah further express their faithfulness to God in the circumstances around their son's birth?
- Zechariah's prophecy after John's birth (Luke 1:68-79) is recited, chanted, or sung as part of daily worship in several Christian traditions. Listen to and/or sing one or more musical settings of this text, including some that may be found in your congregation's hymnal. How does the music reflect and affect your understanding of Zechariah's words?
- How, if at all, does your congregation use extended periods of silence in its worship? How might more or less silence transform your services? If silence is not a regular

part of your worship, talk with pastoral and other worship leadership about whether and how more silence might be incorporated into services.

- Rob mentions the significance of the Temple Mount to Islam. Research the Al-Aqsa Mosque and Dome of the Rock in more detail. If possible, arrange for your group to meet with and learn from someone who is knowledgeable about this site's history and importance in Islam. The conversation should be an opportunity for your group to respectfully listen and learn, not to start arguments.

SESSION 3
NAZARETH
A Place of Simplicity

Session Goals

This session's readings, reflection, discussion, and prayer will help participants:

- Reflect on why God chose Mary of Nazareth to be Jesus's mother.
- Imaginatively enter into the lives of first-century Nazareth and Sepphoris, considering these ancient places as symbolic of contrasting lifestyles, values, and significance today.
- Listen to Mary's "Magnificat" (Luke 1:46-55) for insight into what it means to "carry Jesus within" us today.
- Identify some simple, specific ways in which their lives can become places "the Word [is] made flesh" today.

Biblical Foundations

In the sixth month the angel Gabriel was sent by God to a town in Galilee called Nazareth, to a virgin engaged to a man whose name was Joseph, of the house of David. The virgin's name was Mary. And he came to her and said, "Greetings, favored one! The Lord is with you." But she was much perplexed by his words and pondered what sort of greeting this might be. The angel said to her, "Do not be afraid, Mary, for you have found favor with God. And now, you will conceive in your womb and bear a son, and you will name him Jesus. He will be great and will be called the Son of the Most High, and the Lord God will give to him the throne of his ancestor David. He will reign over the house of Jacob forever, and of his kingdom there will be no end." Mary said to the angel, "How can this be, since I am a virgin?" The angel said to her, "The Holy Spirit will come upon you, and the power of the Most High will overshadow you; therefore the child to be born will be holy; he will be called Son of God. And now, your relative Elizabeth in her old age has also conceived a son, and this is the sixth month for her who was said to be barren. For nothing will be impossible with God." Then Mary said, "Here am I, the servant of the Lord; let it be with me according to your word." Then the angel departed from her.

Luke 1:26-38

And Mary said,

"My soul magnifies the Lord,
    and my spirit rejoices in God my Savior,
for he has looked with favor on the lowly state of his servant.
    Surely from now on all generations will call me blessed,
for the Mighty One has done great things for me,
    and holy is his name;
indeed, his mercy is for those who fear him
    from generation to generation.

Luke 1:46-50

Before Your Session

- Carefully and prayerfully read this session's Biblical Foundations, more than once. Note words and phrases

Nazareth

that attract your attention and meditate on them. Write down questions you have, and try to answer them, consulting trusted Bible commentaries. Become as familiar with these scriptures as possible.

- Carefully read chapter 3 of *On the Way to Bethlehem*, more than once so you are familiar with the content.
- You will need: Bibles for in-person participants and/ or screen slides prepared with Scripture texts for sharing (identify the translation used); newsprint or a markerboard and markers (for in-person sessions).
- If using the DVD or streaming video, preview the session 3 video segment. Choose the best time in your session plan for viewing it.
- If meeting virtually or using a hybrid format, be sure to test your teleconferencing platform and other audiovisual technology before the session.
- *Optional*: Choose pictures or video of the Church of the Annunciation in Nazareth to show the group.
- *Optional*: Select a recording of the musical setting of The Magnificat to which you and your group will listen.
- *Optional*: Select a hymn or Christmas carol related to the Annunciation to read or sing together with your group.

Starting Your Session

Welcome participants. Ask volunteers to react and respond briefly to one or both of these statements from Rob's book. Do they agree? Why or why not? When, if ever, have they found one or both of these statements to be true in their experience?

- "Beginning places are not always good predictors of possibility."

- "[Y]ou can't really tell what is significant about a place (or a person!) by what meets the eye."

Tell participants this session will focus on a place that does appear insignificant, Nazareth. Note, as Rob does, that while modern Nazareth is "a bustling city approaching a population of one hundred thousand people," in Jesus's day it was so "insignificant" we have no first-century references apart from those in the New Testament. Today, however, Christians believe it is the place where the Incarnation—the Son of God becoming a human being—began.

Opening Prayer

Optional: Light the first, second, and third candles (wax or electric) in your group's Advent wreath.

Lead this prayer or one in your own words:

Almighty God, you do not see or judge as we do, for you see and judge the heart. As we study the Scriptures today, open our eyes and our minds to hidden significance. Show us where what is truly meaningful and what truly matters to you are to be found. By your Spirit, may we learn more about how to live in closer alignment with your vision and values, that we, by grace, may play more active parts in the great things you are doing for your people and for the world in Jesus Christ. Amen.

Watch Session Video

Watch the session 3 video segment together. Discuss:

- Which of Rob's statements most interested, intrigued, surprised, or confused you? Why?
- What questions does this video segment raise for you?

Book Discussion Questions

The Annunciation

Recruit volunteers to read aloud Luke 1:26-38, taking the parts of the narrator, Gabriel, and Mary. Tell participants this story is known as "the Annunciation" because Gabriel announced to Mary she would give birth to Jesus. *Optional*: Show pictures or video of the Church of the Annunciation and summarize Rob's description of it.

Discuss:

- As Rob notes, Luke tells us much about Elizabeth and Zechariah's "credentials" to be John the Baptist's parents (1:5-7) but comparatively little about Mary's credentials to be Jesus's mother. What accounts for the difference?
- "Who better," asks Rob, "to carry the life of Jesus within her than someone who could not brag on her ancestry, her heritage, her worth or status, or her accomplishments." How does this lack of a brag-worthy biography make Mary a good candidate to be Jesus's mother?
- Why is Mary "favored" by God (verse 28)? How and why does anyone "[find] favor with God" (verse 30)? Do you feel, or have you ever felt, favored by God? When and why?
- What, specifically, does Gabriel tell Mary about who her son will be (verses 31-35)? Which of these promises do you find most meaningful? Most mysterious? Why?
- Compare and contrast Mary's initial reaction to the announcement she receives from Gabriel (verse 34) with Zechariah's initial reaction to the announcement he receives from Gabriel (1:18). Why do you think their different reactions provoke different responses?

- Why is it important for the reader (verse 26)—and Mary (verse 36)—to know this story takes place in the sixth month of Elizabeth's pregnancy?
- When, if ever, do you find Gabriel's promise, "Nothing will be impossible with God" (verse 37), difficult to believe? Would you qualify Gabriel's promise and, if so, how and why? How, if ever, has Gabriel's promise strengthened your faith or sustained you?

Nazareth and Sepphoris

Before this section of your session, have participants locate Nazareth and Sepphoris on maps of Israel in Jesus's day.

Discuss:

- As Rob discusses, Nazareth in Jesus's day was "seemingly irrelevant" and "virtually unknown." Have you ever been in a place like that? What was the experience like?
- Some who did think about Nazareth, such as Jesus's disciple Nathanael, don't seem to have thought highly of it and its people (see John 1:46). What are some places today from which few, if any, think anything good can come? Why do they have this reputation? How, if ever, have you or your congregation challenged the reputation of one of these modern "Nazareths?"
- Rob conjectures that life in first-century Nazareth "would have been lived at a much slower, less frenetic pace" than elsewhere, or than life in many places today. When have you been in a place where people live life more slowly than you are used to living? What was that experience like, and how, if at all, does it shape the way you live your life?
- Rob posits that the people, and especially the families, of Nazareth supported and depended on each other. Have

you ever been in a place with such a network of neighborly support?

- How much do you and your neighbors support and depend on each other? What about your congregation's neighbors? Are you satisfied with that level of support— and if not, what might you do to start changing it?

- Rob also uses "Nazareth" as a metaphor for any place "we can simplify, reduce distractions, and be free to think." Where is your "Nazareth" in this sense? If you don't have such a "Nazareth," how could you find or create one for yourself?

- Rob contrasts Nazareth with Sepphoris, the "jewel of Galilee." Review the historical information Rob presents about Sepphoris. Where might the modern counterparts of Sepphoris be, and why?

- How would you summarize the differences between the values and priorities of Nazareth and Sepphoris?

- "At one time," writes Rob, "Sepphoris was a place to feel significant, but Nazareth was, in fact, the place to find significance. One had more of a future than the other." Do you think the church has a part to play in making the "Sepphorises" of this world more like "Nazareths?" If not, why not? If so, why, and how does the church go about doing it?

The Value of a Simple Faith

Recruit a volunteer to read aloud Luke 1:46-55, or read Mary's words in unison as a group (provide participants with the same translation from which to read). Tell participants these verses are often called "The Magnificat" because of the first words in their Latin translation ("Magnificat amina mea Dominum," verse 46b).

Optional: Listen together to and discuss a musical setting of The Magnificat you have chosen.

Discuss:

- How does Mary interpret the coming birth of her child? How did Jesus's earthly ministry look and/or not look like what Mary expects?

- Why does Mary say she is in a "lowly state" (verse 48?) When, if ever, have you been—or are you in—a lowly state? How do you think Mary's words sound to those in a lowly state today?

- How do Mary's words connect with God's past history with Israel? How do they point forward to God's future with Israel, and with the world?

- How do your work and your congregation's work in Jesus's name reflect the values in Mary's words?

- "Have you ever known people who carry Jesus within them?" asks Rob. How do you answer? How do you recognize such people? How can we live as such people?

Closing Your Session

Recruit a volunteer to read aloud John 1:1-5, 14 (or read these verses in unison, from the same translation). Remind participants that Rob says the words carved in the altar at the Church of the Annunciation allude, in Latin, to John 1:14: "Verbum caro hic factum est"—"The Word became flesh here."

Read aloud from Rob's book: "The journey to Christmas goes through Nazareth. This is where God's love became specific. At a particular time, to a particular girl, in a particular place, God chose to become flesh."

Tell participants that while the Incarnation described in John 1:14 is unique, God's love can become specific at any time, in any place, in all our lives. Invite participants to spend a few minutes reflecting on a simple way in which someone has made God's love specific for them, and on at least one simple way in which they could make God's love specific for someone else between now and your next session. Invite volunteers to talk briefly about their reflections.

Thank participants for their engagement in this session. Encourage them to read chapter 4 of *On the Way to Bethlehem* before your next session.

Closing Prayer

We praise you, Jesus Christ, Word of God and Light of the World, for entering our life in Nazareth. Keep us alert when you come to us in specific ways today, for there is no place where you cannot meet us, and no one through whom you may not call us to follow and to serve. Amen.

Optional Extensions

- Find and view a wide selection of artwork, from different periods of history and in different styles, depicting the Annunciation. Which of these images seem most compelling to participants, and why?
- Rob mentions the size and activity of Nazareth today. Recruit volunteers to research present-day Nazareth and to report back to the full group at the start of the next session. What further comparisons and contrasts between Nazareth then and Nazareth now can your group make?
- Rob mentions how Emperor Constantine's mother, Helena, sponsored the building of churches throughout the Holy Land. What other churches did Helena build?

What is your opinion of Helena's project to mark and memorialize important Christian sites in this way?

- Protestant Christians frequently consider Roman Catholic devotion to Mary confusing at least and mistaken at worst. Invite someone who is knowledgeable about Marian devotion to speak with your group. The conversation should be an opportunity for your group to respectfully listen and learn, not to start arguments, and should include acknowledgment of what "common ground" Catholic and Protestant Christians share about the mother of Jesus.

SESSION 4
BETHLEHEM
A Place of Humility

Session Goals

This session's readings, reflection, discussion, and prayer will help participants:

- Reflect on how knowledge about and firsthand visits to their "ancestral homes" may have shaped their sense of identity.
- Review the events that took place in Bethlehem in the Book of Ruth, their significance for Jesus's sense of identity, and their ethical implications for Jesus's followers today.
- Put God's promise through Micah to Bethlehem in historical context, to better understand what it meant for Micah's original audience and what it means for Christians today.
- Identify with the Bethlehem shepherds as those who both receive and give blessings.

Biblical Foundation

Now in that same region there were shepherds living in the fields, keeping watch over their flock by night. Then an angel of the Lord stood before them, and the glory of the Lord shone around them, and they were terrified. But the angel said to them, "Do not be afraid, for see, I am bringing you good news of great joy for all the people: to you is born this day in the city of David a Savior, who is the Messiah, the Lord. This will be a sign for you: you will find a child wrapped in bands of cloth and lying in a manger." And suddenly there was with the angel a multitude of the heavenly host, praising God and saying,

> *"Glory to God in the highest heaven,*
> *and on earth peace among those whom he favors!"*

When the angels had left them and gone into heaven, the shepherds said to one another, "Let us go now to Bethlehem and see this thing that has taken place, which the Lord has made known to us." So they went with haste and found Mary and Joseph and the child lying in the manger. When they saw this, they made known what had been told them about this child, and all who heard it were amazed at what the shepherds told them, and Mary treasured all these words and pondered them in her heart. The shepherds returned, glorifying and praising God for all they had heard and seen, just as it had been told them.

Luke 2:8 20

Before Your Session

- Carefully and prayerfully read this session's Biblical Foundation, more than once. Note words and phrases that attract your attention and meditate on them. Write down questions you have, and try to answer them, consulting trusted Bible commentaries. Become as familiar with these scriptures as possible.
- Carefully read chapter 4 of *On the Way to Bethlehem*, more than once so you are familiar with the content.

- You will need: Bibles for in-person participants and/or screen slides prepared with Scripture texts for sharing (identify the translation used); newsprint or a markerboard and markers (for in-person sessions).
- If using the DVD or streaming video, preview the session 4 video segment. Choose the best time in your session plan for viewing it.
- If meeting virtually or using a hybrid format, be sure to test your teleconferencing platform and other audiovisual technology before the session.

Starting Your Session

Welcome participants. Discuss:

- What is or what are your family's place(s) of origin?
- If you've ever traveled to your family's place(s) of origin, what was that experience like? How, if at all, did the visit affect your attitudes about your family?
- If you haven't been to your family's place(s) of origin, would you like to go? Why or why not?
- How do knowledge about and firsthand visits to one's "ancestral home" shape a sense of identity, for better and/or for worse?

Tell participants that this session of your group's study focuses on Bethlehem, the ancestral home of both King David and Jesus.

Opening Prayer

Optional: Light the first, second, third, and fourth candles (wax or electric) in your group's Advent wreath.

Lead this prayer or one in your own words:

Living God, who was and is and is to come: In this time of study, turn our hearts and minds again toward Bethlehem, that as we reflect on your Son's birth there so long ago, we may grow more aware of and receptive to the ways in which he is being born in us, in our community, and in our world today. Amen.

Watch Session Video

Watch the session 4 video segment together. Discuss:

- Which of Rob's statements most interested, intrigued, surprised, or confused you? Why?
- What questions does this video segment raise for you?

Book Discussion Questions

Bethlehem and the Book of Ruth

Recruit a volunteer to read aloud Luke 2:1-5. Remind participants of the political reason Jesus was born in Bethlehem: the Roman census, discussed in session 1. Read from Rob's book: "There is a religious answer [to the question of why Jesus was born in Bethlehem] as well. Joseph had to go back to the place of his ancestral heritage. Joseph was a descendant of David from whom the future Messiah would come."

Have participants turn in their Bibles to the Book of Ruth, which establishes Bethlehem as King David's ancestral home. Do one of the following, as time and your group's biblical knowledge allow:

- Summarize the Book of Ruth, using Rob's summary as a guide.
- Ask volunteers to summarize the Book of Ruth, relying on their previous knowledge and/or skimming the book to jog their memories.

- Recruit volunteers to read aloud these passages for an overview of Ruth: 1:1-18; 2:1-8, 17-20; 3:1-13; and 4:13-17

Discuss:

- Where was Ruth originally from, and how did she come to be a "resident foreigner" in Bethlehem?
- Ruth gleaned grain from Boaz's field in Bethlehem. Read Leviticus 23:22. How does this commandment instruct God's people to provide for those who are poor and strangers in the land?
- Rob notes how Naomi's attitude toward God appears to shift from Ruth 1:20-21 to 2:20. What accounts for the shift?
- What were the responsibilities of a "kinsman-redeemer" in ancient Israel, as seen in the Book of Ruth? (See also Leviticus 25:25.) What parallels to these responsibilities, if any, do you think exist in family relationships today?
- "Just as painful realities can block our ability to see God's hand at work," writes Rob, "the opposite can be true as well. Simple acts of mercy or unexpected blessings can be claimed as evidence of God's love in action." When do you feel you have been most and/or least likely to see God's hand at work in your life or in the world? Have you ever experienced a shift in perspective like Naomi's? What happened to cause it?
- "Sometimes great hope comes in little signs... When our sign of hope doesn't equal the size of our problems, we can walk by an answer to prayer like a penny on the ground, something that doesn't seem worth picking up," Rob writes. Do you agree? Why or why not?

- What would you say to someone who claims to never see evidence of God at work—or who attributes everything that happens to God's hand?
- How does Ruth come to be included among God's people? If Bethlehem is, as Rob states, "where everyone is included in God's provision and hope," where, if anywhere, would you point to as a "Bethlehem" today?
- Why is the fact that King David's ancestry—and, by virtue of being Joseph's legal son, Jesus's ancestry—includes Ruth important?
- Because of the compassion Ruth received in Bethlehem, "Jesus's contains racial ethnicity, immigrant assistance, religious faithfulness, and loving mercy," writes Rob. How much or how little would you say your congregation's "DNA" contains these elements? Your own DNA as a follower of Jesus? Why?

Among the Little

Recruit a volunteer to read aloud Micah 5:2-5a. Discuss:

- What promise does God, through the prophet Micah, make regarding Bethlehem? What makes this promise remarkable or unusual?
- In the eighth century BC, Micah preached both God's judgment against the nation of Judah (the southern kingdom of divided Israel, with Jerusalem as its capital) and its restoration, after a time of exile, in the form of a remnant. Skim the book for examples of both themes in Micah's prophecy. How would this historical context have shaped the way Micah's original audience heard the promise to Bethlehem?

- Read the other most famous passage from Micah, 6:6-8. What connections can you make between it and the promise to Bethlehem?
- Rob writes that Bethlehem, as a "little clan" of Judah, "foreshadowed the many ways Jesus would give attention to those who were among the little in society." He lists some episodes from Jesus's ministry illustrating this attention. What are some others you can add to the list?

Welcoming the Least

Recruit volunteers to read aloud Luke 2:8-20, taking the roles of the narrator, some shepherds (to read the shepherds' words in verse 15 in unison), and the angel. The whole group can read the heavenly host's words in verse 14 together. Discuss:

- Rob explores two views of shepherds in Israel's Scripture: one, as a positive symbol of caring leadership and responsibility; the other, as "people of the land" who were "viewed with contempt." He argues shepherds "possessed a proud identity and noble heritage," but "lived in a world in which others could erode that pride and nobility." What groups of people fit this description in society today? How do you and your congregation act to affirm and preserve their pride and nobility?
- Why, do you think, are the Bethlehem shepherds the first ones to whom angels announce Jesus's birth?
- Who does Rob note were the people *not* at the stable where Jesus was born? Why is their absence significant?
- "The Christmas story reminds us," writes Rob, "that we're all shepherds at heart." What does he mean? Do you agree? Why or why not?

- "God blesses those who recognize their need to be blessed." When have you most recognized your own need for blessing? Did or has God met that need?
- Rob argues the shepherds not only received a blessing but also gave one (verses 17-18). To whom, in Rob's language, might God be "prompting" you to go and bear witness "to the godliness you see in them?" What have or what will you do in response?

Closing Your Session

Read aloud Luke 2:6-7.

Read aloud from Rob's book: "God chose to be born in a manger. God comes to the places where we need God, not where we are doing a pretty good job ourselves keeping life tidied up so things look presentable."

Review some of the "mangers" Rob identifies in society and in individuals' lives. Ask participants to spend a few moments in silence thinking about the "mangers" in their lives where they would most like or most need God to meet them, and to keep these "mangers" in mind as you close the session in prayer (see below).

Unless you are using the optional session 5, thank participants for their engagement in this session, and in the group's whole study of *On the Way to Bethlehem*. Invite volunteers to talk briefly about one key insight they have gained from the study or one question they still have and intend to pursue further.

If you will be using the optional session 5, encourage participants to read the epilogue of *On the Way to Bethlehem* beforehand.

Closing Prayer

God of all places, as our Advent journey brings us at last to the manger in Bethlehem, may we come to see it as not only the place where our Savior was born but also as the place or places in our world and in our lives where we need you the most, and where you have promised to meet us, in your own surprisingly gracious ways. May our spiritual journey to Bethlehem in this season leave us changed, glorifying and praising you wherever we go physically for all you have shown us and done for us in Jesus Christ. Amen.

Optional Extensions

- Find and view a wide selection of artwork from different periods of history and in different styles depicting the angelic announcement to the shepherds of Jesus's birth. Which images appeal most to your group, and why?
- Recruit volunteers to research the Church of the Nativity in Bethlehem and to report back to the full group at the start of your next session (or at some other time, if you are not using the optional fifth session).
- Research further the figure of shepherds in the Bible, beginning with the passages Rob cites (Genesis 46:34; Psalm 23; Isaiah 40:11; Jeremiah 23:3-4; Ezekiel 34:12; John 10:11) and supplementing them with others by consulting a Bible concordance or other trusted resource. How do these passages highlight the difference of opinion Rob sees?

SESSION 5
PERSIA
A Place of Return (Optional)

Session Goals

This session's readings, reflection, discussion, and prayer will help participants:

- Reflect on challenging returns they have had from journeys in the past.
- Identify preconceptions about and traditional misunderstandings of the magi who visited Bethlehem to worship Jesus.
- Explore the difference between returning and "re-turning" (repentance) suggested by the story of the magi and Herod.
- Think about ways in which they have been gifted, and in which they may give their gifts to be of value in other people's lives.

Biblical Foundation

In the time of King Herod, after Jesus was born in Bethlehem of Judea, magi from the east came to Jerusalem, asking, "Where is the child who has been born king of the Jews? For we observed his star in the east and have come to pay him homage." When King Herod heard this, he was frightened, and all Jerusalem with him, and calling together all the chief priests and scribes of the people, he inquired of them where the Messiah was to be born. They told him, "In Bethlehem of Judea, for so it has been written by the prophet:

> *'And you, Bethlehem, in the land of Judah,*
> > *are by no means least among the rulers of Judah,*
> *for from you shall come a ruler*
> > *who is to shepherd my people Israel.' "*

Then Herod secretly called for the magi and learned from them the exact time when the star had appeared. Then he sent them to Bethlehem, saying, "Go and search diligently for the child, and when you have found him, bring me word so that I may also go and pay him homage." When they had heard the king, they set out, and there, ahead of them, went the star that they had seen in the east, until it stopped over the place where the child was. When they saw that the star had stopped, they were overwhelmed with joy. On entering the house, they saw the child with Mary his mother, and they knelt down and paid him homage. Then, opening their treasure chests, they offered him gifts of gold, frankincense, and myrrh. And having been warned in a dream not to return to Herod, they left for their own country by another road.

Matthew 2:1-12

Before Your Session

- Carefully and prayerfully read this session's Biblical Foundation, more than once. Note words and phrases that attract your attention and meditate on them. Write down questions you have, and try to answer them, consulting trusted Bible commentaries. Become as familiar with these scriptures as possible.

- Carefully read the epilogue of *On the Way to Bethlehem*, more than once so you are familiar with the content.
- You will need: Bibles for in-person participants and/ or screen slides prepared with Scripture texts for sharing (identify the translation used); newsprint or a markerboard and markers (for in-person sessions).
- If meeting virtually or using a hybrid format, be sure to test your teleconferencing platform and other audiovisual technology before the session.
- Optional: Gather illustrations of the magi's visit to Jesus, from online sources, books and magazines, and/or old Christian education materials.

Starting Your Session

Welcome participants. Ask:

- When was a time you had trouble coming home from a journey? What happened?
- When, if ever, was a time you had trouble readjusting to your usual routine after a journey? What factors, both within and outside of your control, made your "reentry" challenging?
- What, if anything, would or will you do after your next significant journey to position yourself for "a good return," as Rob puts it?
- Rob's colleague told him he hadn't considered how his own sabbatical changed him when he tried to reenter his usual routine. When and how, if ever, has a journey you've taken changed you in a similar, lasting way?

Tell participants this final session focuses on the magi, "the last visitors to arrive in Bethlehem to worship the Christ Child," and what lessons we can learn from their experience about returning from a spiritual journey.

Opening Prayer

Optional: Add a central candle (wax or electric) to your group's Advent wreath, if it needs one. Light all five candles.

Lead this prayer or one in your own words:

O God, who used the light of a star to lead magi to worship your Son: May the light of your Spirit lead us in this time of study, that we may worship Christ in our reading and thinking, our speaking and listening, and our prayerful reflection, finding in him the place where we most truly belong. Amen.

Book Discussion Questions

The Journey of the Magi, The Original Seekers

Ask participants to brainstorm with you a list of all they know, or think they know, about the magi. Write down responses on newsprint or marker board.

Recruit volunteers to read aloud Matthew 2:1-12, taking the roles of the narrator, the magi, the chief priests and scribes, and King Herod. Review the list about the magi your group has made and identify what things on it are and are not found in the scripture.

Optional: Display artwork that illustrates the magi's visit to Bethlehem, comparing and contrasting it with the scripture. Discuss which image(s) participants like best and least, and why. Ask whether and how such images are helpful even if they differ from Scripture in some details.

Discuss:

• Many Christmas and Epiphany carols notwithstanding,
Scripture doesn't identify the magi as kings. Rob states
the magi were most likely Zoroastrian priests from Persia
(present-day Iran). What significance do you find in
priests from this ancient religion, still a living tradition
today, making a journey to worship the "king of the Jews"
(verse 2)?

• These magi also studied the stars for signs that interpreted
earthly events. Do you give any credence to astrology?
Why or why not? Why would God use a star to lead the
magi to Jesus?

• Rob notes some scholars think the magi arrived as long as
two years after Jesus's birth (see also Matthew 2:16). How
important do you think it is that the magi visited Jesus at a
"house" (verse 11) rather than the stable? Why?

• "Rather than being an irrefutable sign pointing the way
to Bethlehem," asks Rob, "what if [the star the magi
followed] was visible just to those who were seeking?"
How do you picture the star of Bethlehem? Do you think
it is important to identify it with a known astronomical
event? Why or why not? If it was, as Rob suggests it might
have been, visible only to those seeking it, why might the
magi have been looking for it?

• Although he notes the expression has fallen out of favor,
Rob says the term "seekers" can refer to "people who
identify themselves as spiritual but not religious." What do
you understand this distinction to mean? Do you know
someone who is a "seeker" in this sense? Are you such a
"seeker" yourself?

- Rob says "all of us are usually seeking something, if not many things, at any given time." How do your answer Rob's question: "What are you really seeking in your life right now?"
- "Seeking isn't bad," writes Rob, but "it's where our seeking can take us that become problematic." When has your seeking, or that of someone you know, led to problems? Was that problem solved? If so, how? What steps can we take to ensure that in our seeking "we take our yearnings to God?"
- "If our journey includes God, then we must take God's needs, wants, and preferences into account." What does Rob mean? How can we, as individuals and as congregations, discern God's "needs, wants, and preferences" without mistaking them for our own?

Re-Turning versus Returning

Discuss:

- What do you think about when you hear the word "repentance?" What images, memories, and associations does it bring to mind? What, if anything, does the word make you feel?
- As Rob explains, the biblical Greek word for "repentance" is "metanoia," which means "to change one's mind or direction or both." How are the associations of changing mind or direction like and unlike your initial associations with the word "repentance"?
- Rob states "repentance is not a one-time event." Why not? Do you agree?

- Why do the magi, instead of returning to Herod (verse 8), return from Bethlehem to their home country "by another road" (verse 12)?
- How much, if at all, do you think the magi's turn in a new physical direction represents a turn in a new spiritual direction? Why?
- "All Herod did through his whole life," writes Rob, "was keep returning to the same person he had always been. Never did he re-turn and go a different way." Do you think Herod could have repented and "re-turned?" When have you been presented an opportunity to "re-turn" to someone other than you have always been? What did you do? Would you make the same "re-turning" again? Why or why not?
- Who is someone you know who wants or needs to "re-turn" to a new and different life? How can you or your congregation help (or how are you helping) them make that "re-turn?"
- Where is God calling you to "re-turn" in your life today?
- How does or how could your congregation encourage those within and outside of its membership to understand repentance as "re-turning" to a new and different life?

Closing Your Session

Recruit a volunteer to read aloud Matthew 2:13-15. Tell participants that Rob speculates Joseph, Mary, and the child Jesus survived in Egypt for several years by converting the "gifts of gold, frankincense, and myrrh" from the magi (2:11) "into food, clothing, and shelter."

Discuss:

- Rob points to how Joseph and Mary may have used the magi's gifts as "a good reminder of how God uses our gifts far beyond our understanding when we give them." When, if ever, have you been the recipient of a gift that became far more important and valuable than the giver may ever have known? Were you able to communicate that outcome to the giver?
- What are the ways you and your congregation "support the cause of Christ" by giving gifts of treasure, talent, time, and influence? What are some ways you know of that your gifts have made a difference in the lives of others?

Read aloud from Rob's book: "The God who is doing a new thing does new things in us and through us. What has God done for you and how does God want to use that?" Invite participants to spend several minutes reflecting on Rob's questions in prayerful silence. You may wish to ask volunteers to talk briefly about their responses before your group closes in prayer.

Thank participants for their engagement in this session, and in the group's whole study of *On the Way to Bethlehem*. Invite volunteers to talk briefly about one key insight they have gained from the study, or one question they still have and intend to pursue further.

Closing Prayer

Eternal and always active God, you are always bringing about new paths to follow, new opportunities for service, and new life, even if we do not always understand or see how. As our journey to Bethlehem through this study ends, help us to use it as a new beginning, that we may find new ways to be of value in the lives of other people, responding in faith to your great gift of your Son, Jesus Christ. Amen.

Optional Extensions

- Rob alludes to attempts to explain the star of Bethlehem as an astronomical phenomenon. Research some of these explanations. Do they seem convincing to you or not? Why? If astronomers could offer a definitive explanation for the star of Bethlehem, how, if at all, would it affect your faith?

- Challenge participants to return home from your session by a way that is unfamiliar to them, or at least by a way they do not normally go. Urge them to look along the way for opportunities where they might offer their gifts to others—if not right then, then on a return trip! (If you suggest this activity, be sure to take part in it yourself!)

Watch videos based on
On the Way
to Bethlehem:
An Advent Study
with Rob Fuquay
through Amplify Media.

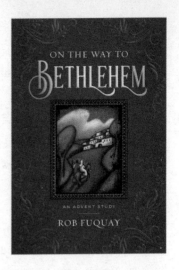

Amplify Media is a multimedia platform that delivers high-quality, searchable content with an emphasis on Wesleyan perspectives for churchwide, group, or individual use on any device at any time. In a world of sometimes overwhelming choices, Amplify gives church leaders and congregants media capabilities that are contemporary, relevant, effective, and, most important, affordable and sustainable.

With *Amplify Media* church leaders can:

- Provide a reliable source of Christian content through a Wesleyan lens for teaching, training, and inspiration in a customizable library
- Deliver their own preaching and worship content in a way the congregation knows and appreciates
- Build the church's capacity to innovate with engaging content and accessible technology
- Equip the congregation to better understand the Bible and its application
- Deepen discipleship beyond the church walls

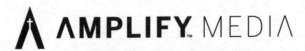

Ask your group leader or pastor about Amplify Media and sign up today at www.AmplifyMedia.com.